Piano Exam Pieces

ABRSM Grade 4

Selected from the 2013 & 2014 syllabus

Name
Date of exam

Contents

Editor for ABRSM: Richard Jones

Other pieces for Grade 4

First published in 2012 by ABRSM (Publishing) Ltd, a wholly owned subsidiary of ABRSM, 24 Portland Place, London W1B 1LU, United Kingdom
© 2012 by The Associated Board of the Royal Schools of Music

Music origination by Julia Bovee
Cover by Kate Benjamin & Andy Potts
Printed in England by Headley Brothers Ltd, The Invicta Press, Ashford, Kent

MIX
Paper from responsible sources
FSC™ C109619

March in E flat

BWV Anh. II 127

from *Clavierbüchlein vor Anna Magdalena Bach, 1725*

Anon.

Clavierbüchlein Little Keyboard Book

This anonymous march is selected from the second of two manuscript keyboard books, entitled *Clavierbüchlein*, that Bach dedicated to his wife Anna Magdalena. The dedication of the second book took place in 1725, perhaps on the occasion of Anna's birthday or else on the couple's wedding anniversary. It became a family album in which Anna evidently collected favourite pieces, compositions by her children, and pieces by visiting musicians.

This march belongs to a group of pieces in the *Clavierbüchlein* to which no composer's name is attached; they were in all probability composed by one of Bach's sons. All dynamics and slurs are editorial suggestions only.

Source: *Clavierbüchlein vor Anna Magdalena Bach, 1725*, Staatsbibliothek zu Berlin, Preussicher Kulturbesitz, Mus.ms.Bach P225

A:2

Scherzo in F

from *Instructive Übungsstücke*

A. E. Müller
(1767–1817)

Instructive Übungsstücke Instructive Practice Pieces

The German composer August Eberhard Müller studied with Bach's second youngest son Johann Christoph Friedrich in Bückeburg and later, in the first decade of the 19th century, held Bach's position as Cantor at the Thomaskirche, Leipzig. Finally, in 1810 he was appointed Kapellmeister at the court of Weimar. He wrote one of the most influential keyboard treatises of his day, the *Klavier- und Fortepiano-Schule* of 1804.

This Scherzo has much of the grace and tunefulness of Mozart, a composer whom Müller greatly admired – earlier, in 1796, he had published a guide to the performance of Mozart's piano concertos. Bar 5 might be played staccato like b. 1, though perhaps with a lighter touch (cf. also bb. 34 and 38). The dynamic *mf* is editorial in bb. 9 and 28, as are the right-hand slurs in bb. 51–6.
Source: *Instructive Uebungsstücke (Pièces instructives) für das Pianoforte* (Leipzig: C. F. Peters, c.1820)

AB 3631

Fine

poco rall.

Tempo
primo

cresc.

D.C. al Fine

Sonata in G minor

Domenico Scarlatti
(1685–1757)

Domenico Scarlatti, Neapolitan by birth, emigrated to Portugal in 1719 and then to Spain in 1728. He spent the rest of his life in Madrid as *maestro de capilla* and music master to the young Princess Maria Barbara, who later became Queen of Spain. Most of his solo keyboard sonatas, well over 500 in number, were composed after his emigration to the Iberian peninsula.

    This sonata, alongside three others, was discovered by Bengt Johnsson in 1984 in the archives of the Escolania de Montserrat (the boys' choir of the Benedictine abbey Santa Maria de Montserrat near Barcelona); it was first published in 1985. The sonata's recent discovery explains why it is absent from Ralph Kirkpatrick's catalogue of the Scarlatti sonatas, which appeared over 30 years earlier in 1953. Its brevity and simplicity suggest that it might have been composed around the time of Scarlatti's first published collection, the *Essercizi* of 1738, or possibly even earlier.

    The sonata requires a *legato cantabile* touch throughout. All grace notes are to be played on the beat, as shown above the stave in b. 2. The right-hand *d*'s in b. 6, the appoggiaturas in bb. 6, 14 and 16, the grace notes in b. 15, and the trill in b. 16 are editorial additions (cf. bb. 4, 7, 8 and 14). All dynamics and slurs are also editorial.

Source: MS copy, archives of Escolania de Montserrat, AM 2158

© 2012 by The Associated Board of the Royal Schools of Music

B:1

The Sun is Setting

William Alwyn
(1905–85)

Slow and expressive [♩ = c.72]

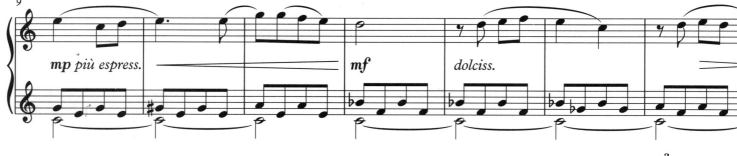

The English composer William Alwyn studied flute and composition at the Royal Academy of Music, where he was appointed professor of composition in 1926 – a post he held for 30 years. In 1927 he took an additional post as flautist in the London Symphony Orchestra. He is well known for his film music, which comprises over 60 scores, including several war-time documentaries.

The Sun is Setting is notable for its haunting melody, which resembles a folksong. The middle section of this three-part piece (bb. 18–37) sounds rather like a solo for the flute. The return of the 'folksong' (b. 38) at first has something of the character of a cello solo, then of a violin solo on the lower strings (b. 46).

AB 3631

B:2

Silta, jauka istabiņa

Arranged by Lūcija Garūta

Trad. Latvian

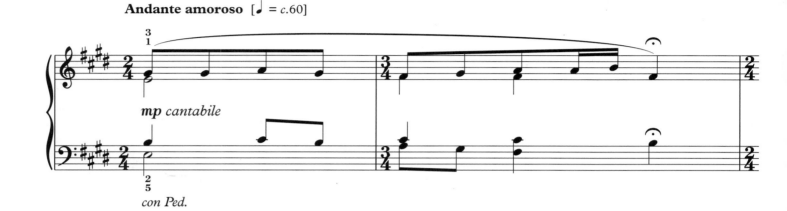

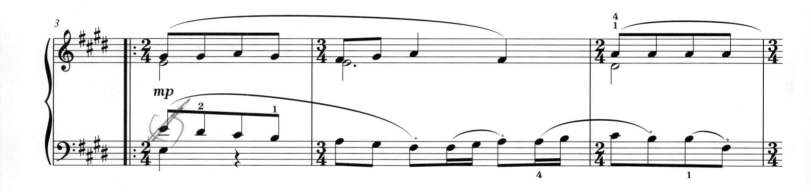

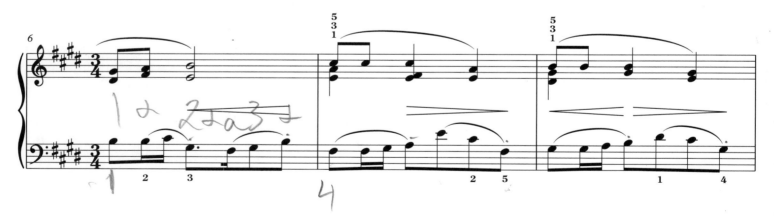

Silta, jauka istabiņa The Warm and Pleasant Room

Lūcija Garūta was a prominent Latvian composer, pianist and teacher who studied at the Latvian Conservatory from 1919 to 1925, and then spent several years in Paris, studying piano with Alfred Cortot and composition with Paul Dukas. She taught at the Latvian Folk Conservatory from 1926 to 1947 and at the Latvian State Conservatory from 1940 till her death in 1977.

Her music is not only Romantic in style but deeply Latvian in feeling, and she made many arrangements of Latvian folksongs. Among them are her *Latviešu tautasdziesmu apdares* (Latvian Folksong Arrangements) for piano, which include the piece selected here. Its words are about love for one's mother: 'The room is warm and lovely, heated by the birch-wood stove. It becomes even warmer and more dear when mother comes into the room!' The addition of *con Ped.* in b. 1 is an editorial suggestion only.

© Copyright Musica Baltica Ltd, Riga, 2007

Reprinted by permission. All enquiries about this piece, apart from those directly relating to the exams, should be addressed to Musica Baltica Ltd, Kr. Barona 39-1, Riga LV-1011, Latvia.

Alvedans

No. 4 from *Lyriske småstykker*, Op. 12

Edvard Grieg
(1843–1907)

Molto allegro e sempre staccato [♩. = *c*.66]

Alvedans Dance of the Elves; **Lyriske småstykker** Lyric Pieces

The Norwegian composer and pianist Edvard Grieg was adept at inventing miniature character-pieces for the piano, many of which were collected in his ten sets of *Lyric Pieces*, published between 1867 and 1901. Angus Morrison, editor of Grieg's piano music for ABRSM, has written: 'The first volume of *Lyric Pieces*, Op. 12 [from which 'Alvedans' is selected] was published in 1867…I think there can be little doubt that [these pieces] were a conscious attempt to provide attractive material for the beginner, somewhat on the lines of Schumann's *Album for the Young*.'

   In this dance, Grieg only marks the first instances of staccato patterns, but it is likely that he intended them to be applied to similar patterns throughout the piece. As an alternative to Grieg's pedalling in bb. 29–30 and 51–2, players might lift and press the pedal at the bar-line.

© 1984 by The Associated Board of the Royal Schools of Music
Adapted from Grieg: *Lyric Pieces & Poetic Tone-Pictures*, Op. 12 & Op. 3, edited by Angus Morrison (ABRSM)

C:1

Ne tirez pas sur le pianiste!

No. 8 from *12 petites histoires*

Emmanuel Oriol
(born 1968)

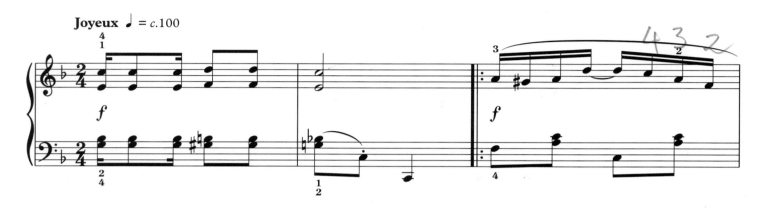

Ne tirez pas sur le pianiste Don't Shoot the Pianist; **Petites histoires** Little Stories

The title of this entertaining piece is a humorous play on the famous 1960 gangster film by François Truffaut, *Tirez sur le pianiste* (Shoot the Pianist), which starred Charles Aznavour in the title role.

Although the composer's metronome mark is ♩ = *c*.100, players may prefer a tempo of ♩ = *c*.88. Either tempo would be acceptable in the exam.

© Editions Francis Salabert

Reproduced by permission of Universal Music Publishing MGB Ltd. All enquiries about this piece, apart from those directly relating to the exams, should be addressed to Universal Music Publishing MGB Ltd, 20 Fulham Broadway, London SW6 1AH.

C:2

La peruanita

from *Piezas para niños menores de 100 años*

Federico Ruiz
(born 1948)

La peruanita The Little Peruvian Girl; **Piezas para niños menores de 100 años** Pieces for Children Under 100 Years of Age

Federico Ruiz was born in Caracas, Venezuela. In his compositions he combines elements of Venezuelan and Latin American popular and folk music with the traditions of mainstream Western art music, including contemporary and atonal music.

'La peruanita' is a Peruvian-style waltz, composed in 1990 and first conceived as incidental music for a play. It was inspired by the innocence and simplicity of a little girl. The character of the music might suggest that the little Peruvian girl of the title is rather lonely and sad (right hand, *legato cantabile*), but she still knows how to dance (left hand, staccato crotchets in waltz rhythm). Her mood lightens and she grows more cheerful when the music turns from the tonic, E minor, to the relative major, G, in b. 17. All dynamics from b. 17 onwards are editorial suggestions only.

Swinging Bells

Poul Ruders
(born 1949)

The Danish composer Poul Ruders studied organ and piano at the Odense Academy, and in 1975 graduated from the Royal Danish Conservatory, Copenhagen. His large output includes opera, orchestral works, chamber music and vocal works.

Of *Swinging Bells* the composer has written: 'Don't let the changing metres deter you – they make the canopy of bells swing and dance, tinkling and clear as crystal.'

Reproduced from *Spectrum 4: an international collection of 66 miniatures for solo piano*, compiled by Thalia Myers (ABRSM)